Samantha's Solar Spin

Contents

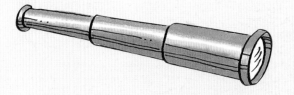

Written by Lizzie Durbin
Illustrated by Trevor Pye

Awake at Night

Samantha was in bed. Her mother had tucked her in and her father had read her a story. Samantha felt sleepy, but she didn't want to go to sleep yet.

At last, she heard her mother and father go to bed. She heard the lights being turned off.

Samantha sat up at once and jumped out of bed. Her grandpa had given her a shiny gold telescope for a birthday present. He'd said it was a very special telescope. Samantha couldn't wait to try it out!

3

Tomorrow, Samantha's class was going to talk about the solar system. Samantha wanted to look through the telescope tonight so she could tell the class that she had already seen the planets.

Samantha held the telescope up to the window and looked through it.

Samantha could see the moon, and she could see the stars.

"How do I know which ones are planets?" she asked herself.

She moved the telescope a little bit. Now she could see a cat running down the street.

Through the Telescope

Then something very strange happened. Samantha's face felt funny, as if it was being squeezed and stretched at the same time.

The telescope was starting to swallow her up! Now Samantha's whole body felt as if it was being squeezed and stretched! The telescope had swallowed her!

9

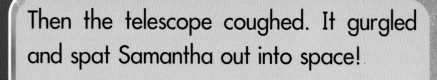

Then the telescope coughed. It gurgled and spat Samantha out into space!

"Wow!" she said.

10

Earth floated far below her. It was blue and green, with bits of white.

Samantha could see the sun and the moon, too. She could see a lot of very bright stars.

"Wow!" she said again.

Journey Through the Solar System

Samantha looked around.

"I'll visit all the planets in our solar system!" she said to herself. "But I'll visit the sun first, because the sun is a star, not a planet!"

She closed her eyes and opened them again slowly.

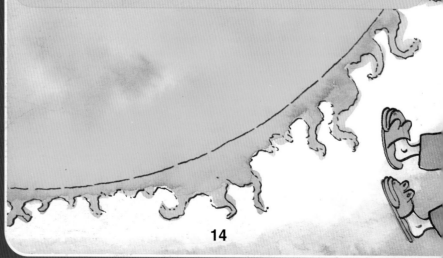

The sun was shining in front of her. Quickly, she closed her eyes again. She couldn't look at the sun. It was too bright!

"It's very, very hot here," said Samantha. "I think I'll go to Mercury."

Mercury was the planet closest to the sun. Samantha closed her eyes again and zoomed to Mercury. Up close, Mercury looked a bit like the moon. It had a lot of craters.

"It's very hot here, too," said Samantha. "It must be because this side of the planet is facing the sun. I'll go and see what Mercury is like on the other side."

Samantha flew across Mercury. She landed on the dark side of the planet, away from the sun. She began to shiver.

"The side of Mercury that faces the sun is very, very hot and the side that faces away from the sun is very, very cold," said Samantha. "I think that I've had enough of Mercury."

The next planet Samantha went to was Venus. Venus was covered in thick clouds, so Samantha couldn't see anything.

"Venus is even hotter than Mercury!" she said. "Am I thirsty!"

But she didn't look for water because there wasn't any on Venus!

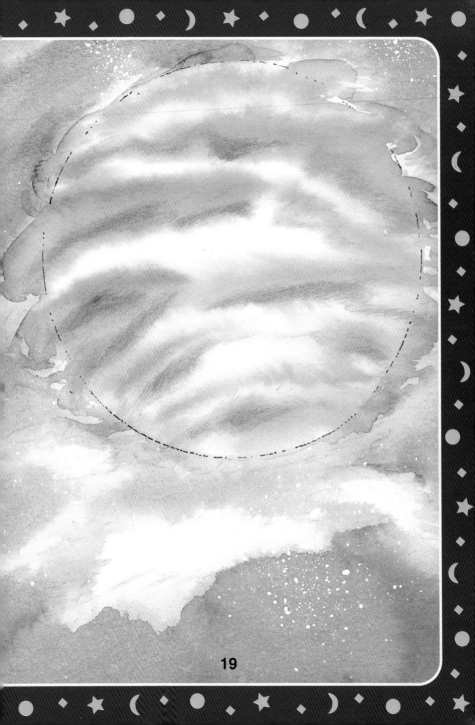

Samantha decided that it was time to go back to Earth to get a drink. With a blink of her eyes, she popped back through the telescope and into the kitchen at home. She had a long drink. Then she squeezed into the telescope again and set off for the moon.

Samantha zoomed around and around the moon. She looked closely at the craters that she'd seen from Earth. In one of the craters, she found a sign that said *Grandpa was here*.

"Grandpa's been here! He must know that the telescope is special," she said. "Next time he tells one of his stories, I'm going to believe him!"

There was a pen by the sign, so Samantha wrote *Samantha was here, too.*

Grandpa was here.

Next, Samantha headed for Mars.

"Mars is very red!" she said to herself as she stood on the top of a big red mountain. She looked down into a big red crater and blinked.

There was Grandpa, waving at her from the other side of the crater!

"Hi, Samantha!" he shouted. "I hope you're enjoying your birthday present! I'll see you at home later!"

Then Grandpa zoomed off in the direction of Mercury, but Samantha went to Jupiter.

Jupiter was huge, bigger than all the other planets in the solar system. Samantha visited two of Jupiter's 16 moons. There were a lot of volcanoes on the moon Io, and Samantha felt hot. She went for a swim in the icy seas of the moon Europa.

Then she zoomed off through the pretty rings to Saturn and Uranus.

Uranus was cold, dark, and green, and the rings were not as pretty as the rings around Saturn.

"Phew, it smells here," said Samantha. "It must be the gas on the planet."

Far Out in Space

There was only Neptune and Pluto left to visit now so Samantha flew over to Neptune, the blue planet. But she didn't stop, and she soon reached Pluto.

She felt very lonely on Pluto, because Pluto was so far away from Earth. The sun was so far away now that it just looked like a very bright star in the sky.

Samantha had had enough, so she closed her eyes and thought of Earth.

31

Home Again

She zoomed through the universe and squeezed herself back through the telescope and into bed.

"I can't wait to tell the class about my trip through the solar system," she said, as she fell asleep.